AF355402

Routes Of Remberance

Kristi Hager Johnson

BookLeaf Publishing

India | USA | UK

Copyright © Kristi Hager Johnson
All Rights Reserved.

This book has been self-published with all reasonable efforts taken to make the material error-free by the author. No part of this book shall be used, reproduced in any manner whatsoever without written permission from the author, except in the case of brief quotations embodied in critical articles and reviews.

The Author of this book is solely responsible and liable for its content including but not limited to the views, representations, descriptions, statements, information, opinions, and references ["Content"]. The Content of this book shall not constitute or be construed or deemed to reflect the opinion or expression of the Publisher or Editor. Neither the Publisher nor Editor endorse or approve the Content of this book or guarantee the reliability, accuracy, or completeness of the Content published herein and do not make any representations or warranties of any kind, express or implied, including but not limited to the implied warranties of merchantability, fitness for a particular purpose.

The Publisher and Editor shall not be liable whatsoever...

Made with ❤ on the BookLeaf Publishing Platform
www.bookleafpub.in
www.bookleafpub.com

Dedication

To Jakeb
Without your love, support,
and encouragement
I would not be where I am today.
I love you my son.

Preface

In *Routes of Remembrance*, the author captures moments in time. Each life carries memories of love and pain, happiness and sorrow. The manifold experiences of the author's life are examined with honest self-exploration. Traversing complex themes of joy, loss, peace, trauma, sickness, growth, and transformation. She has poured her remembrances out upon these pages reminding us that we are all keepers of our own timeline.

Acknowledgements

I would like to thank Local Gems Press for publishing the following poems: *The Overflow, Take, This Tree, and Dear One.* Thank you for giving me the confidence to undertake *Routes of Remembrance.* Thank you to my three adult children – Kara, Jakeb, and Jaret. Loving you has been the greatest joy in my life. Thank you to my husband, Keith, for encouraging me every step of the way and for helping me find my voice again.

The Queen of 4th Street

Pure magic happened when Grampa turned onto Great
Grammy's street.
Brick paved 4th Street in Massillon, Ohio could
wake even the sleepiest cousin.
The house where she lived was magical.
Grampa stood us on the sidewalk trying to give us a
lesson in history.
Across the street the stately Five Oaks built in 1892.
Silent film star, Lillian Gish, had owned a home here.
The bricked street helped put food in bellies during the
depression.
I didn't understand its historical significance then.
I only knew this wondrous road led to her.
She would be waiting for the Faulds tribe to arrive.
Waiting in her chair, her tiny feet propped on a round
ottoman.
Aunt Nan would have just unleashed her tight bun of
silver hair.
She was brushing it with long gentle strokes,
Grammy's eyes were closed. A tiny smile of delight
across her lips.
We children watched as she was laid gently back and the
long hair became
warm and wet silver encased in iridescent floral bubbles.

This was the crown I remember
for she was beautiful this way.
After the rinse came the great pink towel and she would sit
her throne again.
Her eyes would search for me as she patted me to her knee.
Everything would fade away.
It was just her and me.
Those few moments of undivided affection are stored up
in my memory.
My cousins all remember differently.
Baby swiss for a snack, the red sofa with bolster pillows
in the hall,
little and mean, Pico the dog (who dared to bite our
sweet Grammy).
The long porch with the curving stairs where we played.
Pancakes with butter and sugar,
the sound of her bell collection ringing out.
The laughter mixes making the music of family.
Grammy sat, a turbaned queen, reigning over us all.
But, when her hair was dry and coiled back atop her head
it was time for us to gather along the 4th Street's edge.
Wait for Grampa to say his goodbyes and
round up the last cousin for the hours journey home.
I counted the bricks in the street to distract myself.

I remember the red rust, pink, and brown rectangles
with a mixture of fondness and regret -
For they both took me to her palace
and took me away from her again.

The Road

I chose the road most traveled,
though I could have chosen a highway to
irreproachability.
But, the kindness offered to me was, for my part,
simply a trail of tears of another kind.

My road would be the many travelled path of
dark daylight and eyes glowing with censurable
entrapment.
This path, riddled with shallow puddles of tears for
sipping
and scraps of unleavened bread,
turning to ash in my mouth.

Guilt was my guide
with iniquitous veins on a map.
Time dilation through lies.
Signs of every kind, but no sign to direct me.

Every side street called out
to change my route.
Turn here, change, stay the same.
The faster I traveled the most traveled road
the slower I moved misguidedly.

Tell Me

Tell me, tell me true;
Am I enough for you?
A blackout confession ripped forth.
I found myself thrust onto the road to Arras.
His voice atop the waters Seine.
Floating polluted words boiled up from deep deceit.
You insignificant grisette; I want a girl I can pin to my
wall.
Bleach your hair!
Straighten your curls!
Wear make-up and paint yourself into an image I might
desire;
you stupid, worthless doll!
This is Possession Street and I own the whole block -
I own the whole city! I own you!
My ears ached from the boxing of unadulterated truth.
He had told me, told me, told me true.
I had taken refuge in illusions of champagne kisses.
Now free from delusion I saw his mouth for what it was
-

Septic and gaping,
swallowing every lovely thing that was left of me.
In this comedy of tragedy
there were no vows of love and acceptance.

No saviour, no future.
I was Fantine on the Pont au Change
with no Jean Valjean to redeem
the wasted years of naive youth and fictitious dreams.

Stripped Away

I conceive in a dream
the road less travelled
transporting me
through a quiet wood.
All the trees elongated and clean,
blocking out the sun.
The air moving, spinning
without disturbing the sacred grove.
No shadow cast by me,
no shadow cast by tree.
The ground beneath becomes
a river meandering.
No ripple or current, but still
moving me along.
A child's laughter oscillating -
drawing me forth out of hiding.
Am I past, present or future
upon this nameless place?
It is only in the dream state
the answers finally come.
Only this road ever
lead to peace
and it was lost to me.

Aubrey

Our friendship died long before Aubrey did.
The last picture of her you sent was only her silhouette.
Tiny and cold, backpack dragging her down an icy road,
a mountain shrouded in gray rising above her.
You were asking for money again.
Complaining about her being an unbearable load.
She had been safe and warm -
not cared for, but protected at the shelter
till you let your addiction back in.
I never forgave you for choosing it
over your own kin.

I have a photo of her.
I don't keep it for you.
She is two pounds and you are holding her for the first
time.
Your expression is haunted.
I should have seen the nightmare you would cause her
life to be
and promulgated your future crimes
before all humanity.

You texted me -

Aubrey is dead.
Dead, you said - in a text.

I did not know you anymore.
I know now, I never did.
I phoned you because I loved her.
I listened.
Once more taking on your
pain, fear, little remembered joys.
I was numb to your lack of true candor.

That icy mountain morphed before my eyes; I could see
it through my tears.
Her life had been formed in the valley of a frigid mother.
Her death was the climb you forced her to take.
I listened to the lie that you loved her,
and then I said goodbye.

The Path of Grief

She stood her arms stretched to the heavens
as if calling out to God to take her now.
Amidst her husband's internment with everyone around,
her lovely face now a mournful shroud.

He had poisoned himself with alcohol for years.
He could not stop until the hospital.
Could not stop for all her tears.

His room was one reserved for the dying.
I travelled the corridor with woeful dread,
but still trying.

She met me in the hall filled with light.
She was taking him home. Home for one night.
The doctors counted the cost and found
it could not hurt him now.

At sunset, on the emerald bay, the pastor arrived
carrying the Holy Book at his side.
He was baptized in the bathtub, born anew.
Three days later his life on earth was through.

He had planned how his funeral would be.

The flowers, her favorite, white peonies.
The music played, loud and long, on the drums of his
son.
But, he could never have foreseen his five year old down
on her knees.
Throwing petals into the hole where Daddy would now
rest
beside the Sweetgum tree.

I watched from a distance the dreary mass.
People assembled who loved him
despite his self destruction and theirs,
to the very last.

Her effigy remains with me to this day.
A woman alone on a grief stricken path.
Pregnant with loss in the aftermath.

The Way of the Deceiver

I do not know you.
No, not anymore.
Timorously, I assure myself I did at one time.
Ambiguous amnesia floods my mind.

Last night, without direct quotable words,
with a deaf witness in the room,
you told me -
I have ruined your life.
The force of the words upon impact leave
a blood splattered crime scene.

Somehow you have framed me for your life's failure.
I am innocent.
I stand trial unjustly accused.
The decay of your conjured panjandrum
belongs solely to you.

Permeating chaotic mentality
and sociopathic pursuit.
You hunted my impulse for joy
attempting to corrupt and deceive
as you gaslit my vitality.

I am aquitted.
I do not know you;
I have never met this person before.
You and your words, like gasoline, evaporate.
Even now I witness with wonderment as they swiftly
abate.

The Stain

An old chair sat cosily alongside a boy's splintered bed.
A rack of her designer clothes smashed up against dirty
yellow walls.

She had been renowned for her style and flair.
Her red lipstick and her beautiful blonde hair.
She was a lady in every sense of the word.
But, now the inheritance she left to her daughter seemed
absurd.

Hidden amongst the couture labels,
a baby pink hoodie.
At the neck a dry white stain of some kind.
Soft and warm and comfortable like her.
Could this have been what she actually preferred?

There's more behind this door.
More?
Door?
My fingers reached to touch the crusty stain,
resisting the urge to scratch it away.

I recoiled that possessions once so tenderly kept
could be left like orphans in a storm.

Was the stain chicken salad sandwiches with Ann?
Coffee creamer and a shaky hand?
Strawberry milkshakes after pool time with the
grandchildren?

I will take it - I say greedily.
But, I won't be able to wash it away,
for fear of losing her and all the memories of those
lucent days.

Pain

Ride in, abhorred acidic adversary,
on ashen waves of pain.
Conquering my body.
Sifting thoughts through an icy, steel sieve.
Allowing the nightmares to catch
but, the snippets of truth slip.
Trapped in a wormhole of haze and blaze.
I hear the vicious impetus, like a steam train whistle,
conducting me.
Bidding me come.
Come instantly.

Frozen hands and feet,
fevered brow.
Needle stabbing through socket and eye -
driving deep into the bone on the opposite side.

Cracking, grinding, feebly trying to disentwine from
the dreaded blue orb,
which lights both day and night,
interchangeably.

Oh cold, hateful, familiar companion -
I am riding into isolation again.

Though I fear your answer I still implore,
When will you tire of tormenting me?
I hear you hiss villainously.
Close my eyes,
drop my pen,
only to surrender - unwillingly - again.

Blossom Bandits

The morning sea fog rolled in overnight
causing the spring pine pollen
to cling to my window panes.
The sound reached my ears first;
a frenzy of soprano trills.
Through flaxen looking glass I spied
statuesque apple trees transform with life.
Green and pink to brown-gray and yellow.
Alive with fluttering trespass.

I crept to a place where the fog had dripped a clean trail.
Bewildered, I watched a mad flock of Cedar Waxwings
gorge upon my precious apple blossoms.
I tapped on the glass with my mug of oolong tea,
but the birds did not budge. They simply ignored me.

The migrating bandits must have been half starved
flying over the Isle of Pines.
The flock was more concerned with empty bellies,
now replete with soft petaled breakfast,
than with my trying to shoo them away.

Pixie dust pollen began to flutter upon each wingbeat
as the birds continued to forage and feast.

Their crests ruffled gleefully atop their heads.
Harmoniously, they took a deep audible breath.
A moment of silence before the next cacophony of song.

Dipping and diving,
little thief faces,
black beaks stuffed full of sweet delicacies.
I watched with helpless wonder and heard my own
laughter
ring out joining their choir.
I realized there would be
no apple picking this year or next.
These clever masked bandits would remember their
route.

Even the fallen petals were devoured and
with one last Baroque trill they simultaneously took to
flight.
Leaving behind innocent transgress.
My trees stood,
sheets of noteless music,
each branch an empty bar.
Only the scarlet dots of innumerable wings could be seen
as they topped the pines at incredible speed
resuming their skyfaring exodus.
I was glad my flowers had met their need.

They had left me a memento - having truly been
blessed by this indelible scene.

Northern Lights

My daughter called after eleven that night.
Go outside, you can see the Northern Lights!
I can see them here in Colorado!
I could hear the watery crinkle of her smiling eyes; her
voice beamed -
I never thought I would ever see anything so lovely!
I protested about being in my jamies
already in bed.
Once in a lifetime - she said.
I walked out past the floodlights hiding
the sky from my sight.

I had once guided her through lessons in nature.
Now, she piloted me through my own North Carolina
backyard,
my very own conveyor -
Go out beyond the big oak tree!
Look through your camera lens.
Point it north - she giggled.
We shared the secret joke, like we do,
of people who can't figure things out and haven't a clue.

I felt my way through the dark
past the old tobacco barn.

My eyes filled with wonder,
over the cottonfield the sky was shimmering ruby red.
I see it - I whispered sacredly to my child
two thousand miles away from me.

My camera captured a crimson sky ablaze with
enormous diamond stars.
All displayed upon vermillion silk for my pleasure.
As I described what I saw to her
the hairs stood up on both of our arms.
We were silent then.
Realizing at once, simultaneously, we were still together
under the night heavens.

The homesick ache in both of us receded.
We could and would continue to experience
precious, priceless moments together.
We described, in detail, the Northern Lights to one
another
until our phones began to say low power.
Call me back when you get inside. You know,
I would pick you to be my mother in any lifetime.

No matter the distance,
no matter the time -
We are still sharing firsts in a life divine.

Crossroad Prey

Reckless and deliberate you picked up a hitchhiker
thumbing a deserted road.
You knew I was afraid
for I had begged.
He smelled of sweat and alcohol
but, you kept him just the same.
You drove for miles
to the next town,
a stranger in your car.
I pressed myself to invisibility against the door,
kept my hand on the handle
in case I had to leap,
and prayed.
You watched me,
side eyed, and beat me without your fists.
Let me know my life held no more value to you
than the beat up old car you drove.
You only let him out because he lit a cigarette in the
back.
Hissing at me to crack the window
you decided my punishment was through.
In silence you drove off leaving the stranger behind.
I watched him in the mirror,
fade to a dot on the side of the road,

and wished I could escape this captivity.
I had finally glimpsed the crossroad of my life
at the intersection of Prey and Foreshadow
but, you had locked all the doors.

Granny's Old House

Chartreuse leaves of the dogwood trees
streaks of tangerine
mingle with the darkening sky.

Cotton fields erupting with white
catching the fire,
dark green leaves streaked with mauve shiver.

Cool breeze gently blowing autumn
down this country road
we sit on our new porch watching.

Granny's old house catches last light
remnants of orange,
emerald, rosey pinks, and blues.

I imagine the people who
built the one room house
lived there a hundred years ago

Resting, rocking at days long end
feeling same sense of
grateful calm for September rains.

Looking forward to harvest time
green bonnet head bent
white apron catching ecru balls.

Stiff fingers throbbing long days work
supper to ready
biscuits in the potbelly stove.

Listening to the tangerine
leaves fall to the ground
children under a patchwork quilt

Tapestry of autumn plenty
the colors of life
How different are those bygone years.

The things which remain eternal
kaleidoscope dusk
and cotton fields ripe for picking.

Don't Be Afraid

You clung to your baby years contentedly.

After your evening bath,

warm and drowsy,

lying on a fuzzy rug.

Your crocheted blanket in one hand,

my big toe in your other,

you would drift off to dream

your baby dreams.

You clung to your little one years cheerfully.

In the late afternoon

we took a snuggy.

I stroked your soft little eyebrows while

you gently gripped the thumb of my hand

and held your now named "Little," in the other.

Peaceful, serene I memorized each moment.

On your tenth birthday you told me proudly,

Only eight more years, Mom.

Not Mommy or Momma. Mom.

That night, as the clouds passed over the crescent moon,

I planned my own covert operation to see if,

somewhere in this boy, was my little baby.

I opened the door to your room just a crack.

The night light illuminated your eyes - wide open.

I'm having bad thoughts Momma… Help me.

I told you of Jesus feeding the crowd with the loaves and
fishes.
Most importantly I told you how He felt and why He
could not
just send the people away - Jesus knows. Jesus knows.
Don't be afraid - I said with seven kisses.
You either Mommy. Jesus knows.

Incessant Spirits

Empty glasses, bottles,
promises.
I have been here before
in this place
shattering like crystal
chalices
against a concrete wall
bleeding out.
Somewhere in the puddle
lies my dead
pride alongside crushed hope.
I have died
this same death, this same way
many times.
Broken and immunized.
Guaranteed
I would never permit
an encore,
but it it always comes back
taking more.

Tribute Dream

I visited her.
Climbed the stairs.
Felt the scratchy, mottled carpet under bare feet,
and warm light as I rested my chin
upon the window's cool sill at the halfback landing.
Knew the dusty smell of sunlight.
Turned to climb the last four.
She was there.
Tenderness swept over.
Peeling back layer after layer, till like a child,
I knelt at her feet, touched her knee,
felt the softness of her hands when
she bequeathed me
books of flowers.
Favorite pages marked with golden ribbons
emblazoned with strands of light.
I never knew until I went to her, dreamlike,
the tranquility of alikeness
akin to oneness.
This manifestation is a mirror.
I see as eyes cannot, compared by lamplight to an
albumen print,
the sameness.
With diminutive reckoning recall

glimpses of tenderest truth.

She let every clover thrive and dandelion bloom.

Gifted me dreams from heaven

imparting me with transcendent authenticity.

One day I will press the weeds of The Promised Land

into her dear hands.

Henbit, chickweed, wild violets,

clover and dandelions ~ a bouquet of tribute.

And at her dear knee

look up into her face thankfully.

Red Flag Warning

Sinking, not proverbial quick sand,
my feet in the ocean before a hurricane.
The tide pulling
the sand ripping
engulfing my feet.
No little shells
just soft sand
transformed into billions of bullets.
The waves froth like a rabid dog.
The color makes me sick,
a churning brown green
algae in a blender.
I feel the strength of the storm
I know the destruction
I have seen the path it takes.
I am paralyzed by the high seas sucking.
My feet are buried
deep, deep, deeper.
Waves come.
Come so strong they bend
me back, a dry reed,
at the waist
splashing bile in my mouth.
I taste all my future tears.

I weep.
No one sees.
The rip current flag is out
and the beach is as desolate as me.

Slave Woman

The star fought to carry the weight of the cloud
pitching and reeling against its burden.
How too am I like that star?
Cloudy night shadowing full moon,
blinking down upon pen and paper.
I write blind -
No more able to see my own words
than sister star knows what
she is beholden to carry across the sky.
Unyielding - we both blaze on drearily for
in our destiny we must observe and be observed.
Tonight's August seabreeze brings
crushed crabapple blossoms and pungent ginger lily
as the star bears its load northward.

I have lived across the Ohio River
at the birthplace of the Olentangy,
in a valley surrounded by mountains,
upon the red clay piedmont among the great oaks -
in the middle of my life by the sea.
Ever my skin tastes of salt,
my hair curls of seaborn breeze,
my body is sunburnt -
I hear the ocean calling to me.

The beauty of these places is my solace
when I cannot contain the cruelness of men.

No matter where.
They are ready to serve themselves up to feast.
What honor among men?
Their breath wreaks of liquor,
their hands rake and burn
like burs of cotton,
tobacco bleeding through - curing, forgotten
drying dead in the barn
waiting to be sold.

Women are poor common useful objects.
They no longer see the stars.
They hide on full nights from
God, Jesus, and the Holy Ghost.
They know gentlemen's sports
are barbarism and rape,
not billiards and darts.

I can barely remember the way to my Ohio River.
I sit, warm nights, in the Carolinas
strangled by her jasmine.
Longing for the smell of snow
breathing in deep
exhaling every drop towards

the caught star
the wagon star
to take this slave woman home.

The Giraffe

The clock was running out of time
at Renschville Elementary.
The playground was where I sat to mourn,
under a shady tree,
while children played ball and tag
I sat solitary.
Art class with ceiling to floor windows.
I could be an introvert
there no one questioned
a child struggling with griefs innuendo.
Concentration, the perfect bend,
wire conforming to eight year old hands.
Paper strips, globs of flour glue,
yesterday's news ripped into strips.
Teacher had forgotten to remove the obits.
There was *her* face
black and white
words formed there about her short life.
Tears shaped but I pushed them aside
and listened obediently as I always tried.

The terrestrial mammals ossicones
should be remembered
along with its long neck bones.

Bones.
I had heard someone say how her face
had been crushed upon the road
that day.
Little austere words stuck to wet eyelashes.
Make the bend, control the insides.
The neck will be long to see above
with wide eyes, ears to hear, and a...
I forgot when the bell rang.

One day to shape, one night to dry.
First light brought a soggy pillow
lashes affixed from grief's sorrow.
The move to Tennessee was coming.
Progenitors' clock would not rewind.
Must finish the giraffe on time.

A mucilage cemetery of
epitaphs, of minute and hour hands.
I was frozen in granite on the last day.
Paint a yellow coat,
fringe the tail,
brown paint for spots...
Mother is here to pick you up.
Try to find the words at eight to say goodbye.
Curiously, I formed them for the old tree -

Thank you for consoling me.
Poor poor child
no time to dry.
It's ok I'll leave the giraffe behind.

Halfway to Tennessee my heart began to heave.
Between rush and grief
I had forgotten to give my creation his mouth.
Going forward, left behind
always stuck within my mind
an estuary of despair
followed me
from there to here.

Jakey

Crust and mantle
rubbing
    rubbing
        rubbing
brain swollen, flooded
until the cerebral fluid
leaks
out her aching left ear.
The boy comes
calling softly -
Mama, you okay?
It hangs too long in the air -
she sees him in double digits
wise beyond his years.
Mama...
She answers using his love name,
lifts one hand,
shaking violently.
She moans, deep guttural.
He clasps her whole arm against his small chest.
Protectively
collapsing over her
while the rest of the fluid leaks

from her eyes
silently.

Apple Pie &

He cornered me in the pub.

The smell of pipe tobacco hung in the air between us.

Twenty-six familiar letters clung to the smoke.

The message mattered not, they simply disappeared.

I lay on them at night trying to remember.

Disbelieving his form absent.

Craving the elixir of mingled breath.

Remembering the pangram of promises, oaths, vows.

Drifting to sleep.

Dreaming of a book I used to know.

Apple Pie ABC

Z - dream of it.

The twenty-seventh letter came

&

and that, per se,

was all it was a story

and no more.

www.ingramcontent.com/pod-product-compliance
Lightning Source LLC
LaVergne TN
LVHW021304200726
843509LV00012B/1772